I Knead
My Mommy

....

AND OTHER POEMS BY KITTENS

I Knead My Mommy

AND OTHER POEMS BY KITTENS

BY FRANCESCO MARCIULIANO

CHRONICLE BOOKS
SAN FRANCISCO

Library of Congress Cataloging-in-Publication Data available.
ISBN: 978-1-4521-3291-4

The following photos © copyright Photographer/iStockphoto: luoman, 2 (typewriter); mjp, 6; KariHoglund, 13; annadarzy, 14; Dixi_, 19; annadarzy, 22; jaimaa85, 27; irontrybex, 28 (kitten); herkisis (frames) 28, 40, 45, 76, 82, 98; RealCreation, 31; Talaj, 36; BSANI, 42; michellegibson, 45; JanPietruszka, 46; jclegg, 49; Iriza, 51; alexxx1981, 53; Stuphipps, 56; Vampirica, 61; Dorin_S, 71 (kitten on stairs); ronen, 75; Lynchian, 76; MikeEpstein, 81; Lilun_Li, 82; prejak, 88; tonisalado, 95; AS_Fotos, 98; gitusik, 100; sansara, 105. The following photos © copyright Photographer/Shutterstock: maturos1812, 2 (yarn); Hasloo Group Production Studio, 10-11; schankz, 17; Orhan Cam, 33; Tom Gowanlock, 38-39; Jorge Pereira, 40; trainman32, 63-64; dien, 65; S-F, 66; Abel Tumik, 69; marekuliasz, 71 (stamp); marslander, 72; TuTheLens, 85; Shebeko, 86-87; Mike Flippo, 93; Nixx Photography, 96; John Smith Design, 103; Ostanina Ekaterina, 108; Andrey_Kuzmin, 111. 5 © copyright Francesco Marciuliano. 36 © copyright 123RF/Elena Kovalena.

Manufactured in China

Designed by Emily Dubin

10 9 8 7 6 5 4 3 2 1

Chronicle Books LLC
680 Second Street
San Francisco, California 94107
www.chroniclebooks.com

DEDICATED TO

Fluffy and Ginger,

two beautiful kittens my parents took in,

and to all the stray cats that need

a loving home.

CONTENTS

INTRODUCTION

Unbelievably adorable. Exceptionably inquisitive. Overwhelmingly energetic. Presently drenched in your sixty-year-old Scotch. Currently sticking its head out of the middle of the birthday cake you made but had yet to serve. At this very moment holding the cord of the ceiling fan, making a wider and wider circumference of shelf-high book/vase/keepsake destruction before letting go and slamming claws-first into your face with the full force of its love as you slowly count to ten before saying, "You . . . are . . . so . . .cute" into its belly.

These are the words people use to describe their kittens. But how do kittens describe their people? Their kitten experience? Their kitten hopes, their kitten concerns, even their kitten selves? Well, thanks to a highly esteemed team of writing instructors who somehow managed to secure an art grant despite submitting a proposal that included the words "kittens," "laptops," and "blank verse," kittens everywhere can now give full expression to their thoughts through the undeniable power of poetry.

From their first toy that was never meant to be their first toy to the lasting pride that comes from going into something that sort of resembles a litter box, from the joy of moving into their forever home to the thrill of forever redecorating that home, these kittens' poems will show you the world as seen through their eyes, and through their hearts, and as they try to pass through a toilet paper tube only to have their head stick out one side and their butt stick out the other, making them look like a kitty cannoli.

Yes, by reading this very collection of their greatest work, you will finally understand why kittens are so inquisitive, where they get their energy from, and, of course, how much they love you. And so maybe the next time your own kitten cuts a swath of destruction through everything you hold dear (but can no longer actually hold because it's all now in pieces) you will be able to look at him or her and say, "I see where you're coming from now. I truly do. I just can't see anything else because you're still holding on to my face with all your claws."

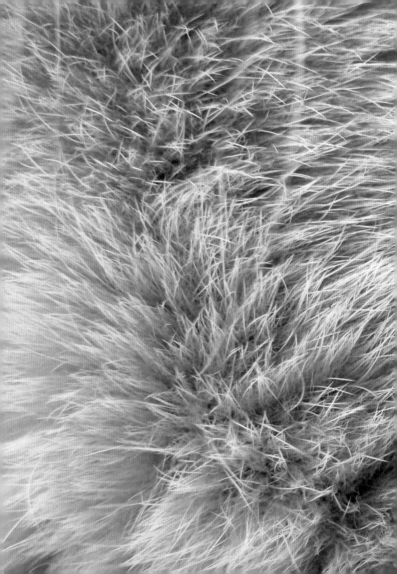

NEW WORLD

When you open your eyes

For the very first time

Try not to look horrified

You might insult a nearby person

KITTEN MAXIM

I Knead My Mommy

. . . .

"Are you my mommy?" I ask
As I knead the blanket
Only for the family quilt
  to lie on the bed

"Are you my mommy?" I ask
As I knead the sweater
Only to find that cashmere
  is so easy to shred

"Are you my mommy?" I ask
As I knead the dog
Only to learn that apparently
  that is not a teat

"Are you my mommy?" I ask
As I knead the chicken
Only for two cutlets to now be
    stuck to my feet

"Are you my mommy?" I ask
As I knead your body
Only to remove clump after clump
    of chest hair

"You are my mommy!" I say
As I keep clawing your skin
Until I get bored and just
    tear into your chair

My Name Is

My name is "Fuzzles"

My name is "Nutters"

My name is "Fuzzles"

My name is "Nutters"

My name is finally "Fuzzles"

My name is finally "Nutters"

My name is a point of contention

Between two little sisters

Until their father steps in

And in the spirit of compromise

Dooms me forever

To be known as "Fuzznuts"

I've Been Watching

Like a human baby

I cry a lot

Like a human baby

I need your help

Like a human baby

I crave your love

Like a human baby

I sometimes wedge myself behind
   the fridge

Or run screaming across
   the kitchen countertop

Or hide inside pillowcases

Only to claw wildly at your ears
   when you rest your head

Like a human baby

I don't know everything about human babies

Especially since you don't have one yet

But when you do

You can thank me for how I prepared you

For when your human baby starts gnawing
  on exposed wires

Ode to a Lizard I Didn't Know
Is Also a Pet in This House

AUUUUUUUUUUU

UUUUUUUUUUUU

UUUUUUUUUUUU

UUUUUUUUUUUU

UUUGGGGHHHH!!!

I'm sorry!

I didn't mean to startle you!

I'm sorry!

I didn't mean to climb the wall!

I'm sorry!

I just had no idea you live here too!

But let's make amends

And let's be best friends

And let's see how much louder

We can make our person scream

By both crawling up his leg at 3 a.m.

My First Toy

. . . .

My first toy

Has wood for me to claw

My first toy

Has string for me to bite

My first toy

Has a hole for me to hide in

My first toy

Is called "Oh dear God, no! My guitar!"

My first toy

Is the best toy of them all

People Food

· · · · · · · · · · · · · · ·

If you leave food on the counter

It's public domain

If you keep food in a bag

It's fair use

If you have food on your plate

It's free license

If you hold food in your hand

It's nonexclusive

And if you open a box of pizza

It's open source

Or crowdsourcing

Or whatever you call it

When my butt plops in tomato sauce

And your head drops in your hands

Perspective

From this very top branch

From the very pinnacle of my world

I look upon my dominion

I gaze on all of which I am king

I see your knee

Pass right by at eye level

And once more I am reminded

That this carpet tree and I

Still have a lot of growing up to do

Curious

· · · · · · · · · ·

Intrigued

Inquisitive

Fascinated

Captivated

Spying

Prying

Curious

This is who I am

This is how I live

This is why I'm now covered

In flour, fudge, and Scotch

Big Box

. . . .

I don't like this big box, I cry

I don't like it at all

There's just too much space

And the sides are way too tall

I don't like this big box, I whine

It feels more like a trap

I miss the coziness of the box of tissues

Or the sticky one with clear wrap

I don't like this big box, I plead

I don't feel quite secure

Anyone can jump in

My ceiling's an open door

I don't like this big box, I yell

How I'll escape I don't know

Then suddenly you lift me out

And I jump back in because I decide when
  and where I go

When I First Open My Eyes

When I first open my eyes
I expect to see marvels
When I first open my eyes
I expect to see splendor
When I first open my eyes
I expect to see
These four other damn fur balls
Who keep pushing me out of the way
To get to mom's milk
Adopted and out of the picture

Not Prepared

. . . .

HOLY—!

WHAT THE—!

SON OF A—!

That thing isn't cute!

That thing isn't purple!

That thing isn't fabric!

That thing isn't at all

Like the toy mouse you got me

Now he's skittering across the floor

Now I'm scrambling up your legs

Now you might as well have me fixed

Because my manhood is as good as gone

Shy Kitten

. . . .

And then another friend shows up
And kisses me as I fidget

And then another friend shows up
And pets me in the wrong direction

And then still another friend shows up
And chases me around the house

And then all your friends
Ask to see your new kitty
And then I wish you were a hoarder
Because I'd like to hide behind
  137 toasters right now

What Will I Be?

. . . .

As a little kitten

I ask my older resident cat

"When I grow

What will I be?

Will I be a guard cat?

Will I be a police cat?

Will I be a rescue cat?

Will I be a seeing-eye cat?"

This is what the older resident cat

Said to me

"YAWWWWWWWWWWN"

Then he rolled over and went back to sleep

Apparently our kind

Is not so professionally inclined

Praise

· · · · · · · ·

All the praise

All the kisses

All the treats

All the love

You give me

For finally using the litter box

All that makes me look forward to

All the applause and awards

You'll give me

When I manage to hit

A much smaller target

Another Way

. . . .

Before I stop squirming

Before I stop screaming

Before I stop trying to remove

Every layer of your skin

Before you

Before the doctor

Before the nurse

All gang up

To hold me down

All I want to say

Is that this is NOT where I saw you

Put the thermometer

When you took your own temperature

Black Kitten

. . . .

I purr

I nuzzle

I lick

I cuddle

I run

I leap

I play

I sleep

But if you think all that is an evil omen

If you think all that is pure bad luck

Then yes, you will endure great misfortune

Because without me your life will suck

NEW FAMILY

If you ever forget

Your person's name

It's either "Chair" or "Sofa"

Depending on their position

KITTEN TRUISM

I Will Save You

. . . .

MEOW MEOW MEOW MEOW MEOW MEOW

DON'T YOU WORRY!

SCRATCH SCRATCH SCRATCH SCRATCH SCRATCH

DON'T YOU FEAR!

BANG BANG BANG BANG BANG BANG

DON'T YOU THINK

FOR ONE SECOND

THAT I WILL EVER STOP!

THAT I WILL EVER GIVE UP!

THAT I WILL EVER LEAVE YOU BEHIND

THIS LOCKED BEDROOM DOOR!

FOR I WILL SAVE YOU

FROM ANOTHER SLEEPLESS NIGHT WITHOUT ME!

Wet

. . . . .

First I get my tongue wet

Then I get my chin wet

Then I get my paw wet

Then I get my head wet

Then I'm soaking wet

Then I'm burning mad

Then I'm wearing it like a turtle shell

Then I'm telling myself that

Next time I'll read the instruction manual

Before I try to drink milk from a bowl again

There Is an Older Cat

There is an older cat

Who does not want me here

There is an older cat

Who hisses when I approach

There is an older cat

Who eats my food

Who steals my toys

Who pushes me off chairs

Who bats me on the head

Who bites me on the neck

There is an older cat

Who does not know

Just how big my breed gets

But there is an older cat

Who in six months' time

Is going to learn that 24/7

Hello!

. . . .

"Hello!"

And you wake up screaming

"Hello!"

And you nick yourself shaving

"Hello!"

And you spill coffee on your groin

"Hello!"

And you fall down six steps of stairs

"Hello!"

And you smash your head on the front door

Every morning when I leap out of nowhere

And meow "Hello!"

You do something so very, very funny

That I'm reminded once more

How lucky I am

To live with someone with such great

comedic timing

Luxury

. . . .

These

These

These right here

Are the softest

Are the comfiest

Are the most luxurious

Bed sheets

I've ever hacked up on

Thank you again for inviting me into your home

And Then You Said "No"

And then you said, "No!"

And then I looked at you

Waiting for a definition

And then you said, "No!"

Again

As if "No!"

Defined the word "No!"

"No! No! No!"

And then I realized

You must be practicing a musical note

Over and over again

"Nooooooooooooo!"

And then I went back

To shoving my paw in your mayo

My Kitten Brother

My kitten brother

My kitten best friend

My favorite kitten

With whom I've shared

Every great kitten adventure

Two great kittens could ever have

Is apparently a schnauzer

But I won't tell him that

For it would break his kitten heart

Secure Room

. . . .

I can hear the resident cat

Sniffing

Scratching

Scrambling to reach

Under my closed door

But before he can enter

I have to feel more secure

I have to build up my courage

I have to perfect my "insane eyes"

Because when we first meet

I want the resident cat to think

"Damn, he crazy!"

And just cede the entire couch to me outright

I'm Right Here

Just because I'm a kitten

Just because I don't say a word

Just because no one else is here

Just because I'm not even looking at you

Doesn't mean you have just cause

To do whatever you want

As if you were all alone

I'm just saying because

If you shove that finger

Any further up your nostril

It's going to get stuck on the second knuckle

Forfeit

. . . .

Remember that time?

That first time?

That glorious

Magical

Wonderful time

When I begged and begged and begged

And you gave in to me?

Yeah

You might as well have signed over

The lease to your house to me that day

x _____

Please Stop

. . . .

I am

I am

I still am

Sigh, yes I am

For a fifth time

That would be me

So I'm begging you

Please stop asking

"Who's a fuzzy, funny fur face?"

Because you're sounding less like

A loving pet parent

And more like

The most unprepared job interviewer

   on the planet

Looking Good

. . . .

Lick

Lick

Slobber

Lick

Lick

There

Now all your left arm hairs

Point in the same direction

And glisten

And smell of seafood surprise

And you're welcome

Now I Know

. . . .

The first time you clipped my nails
I thought, "This person is a maniac!"
The first time you cleaned my teeth
I thought, "This person is a lunatic!"
The first time you gave me a bath
I thought, "This psychopath must be stopped!"
The first time you lovingly brushed my fur
I thought, "Great
Now I feel guilty
For having shoved all those things
   in your mouth while you slept"

Let Me Count

I love you!

I love you!

Let me count the reasons that I love you!

One, you are so kind

Three, you are so warm

The Letter Q, you are so giving

Ampersand, you are so . . .

Let me instead counter

By saying I'm only a kitten

And so my counting skills are not up to par

But from a scale of one to a hundred

Know that my love for you

Is easily exclamation point!

Pretty Kitty

There's a little red bow in my hair

There's a flowery hat on my head

There's a pink frilly dress on my body

There are plastic pearls around my neck

There's like a hundred stuffed animals
  around me

There's a little girl pouring me pretend tea

There's an open door

There's the one chance

For this fluffy kitty to escape

To dye her fur black

And to rename herself "Destroya"

NEW ADVENTURES

Never look back

You'll only appear responsible

For what broke behind you

KITTEN MOTTO

Pass the Time

One day

One long

Slow

Boring

Day

Just to pass the time

I tried licking myself

Down there

Now several hours have passed

Or maybe several weeks

And I feel like I should stop

At least to get something to eat

Or look up to see if you guys still live here

2'6"

2'4"

2'2"

2'0"

1'8"

1'6"

1'4"

1'2"

1'0"

PAWS
116523

Everywhere I Look

There's a bird in a nearby cage
There are fish in that tank
There's even a mouse-like thing
Running around on a little wheel
There's the fast beating of my heart
There's the big lump in my throat
There are the tears of joy in my eyes
As it dawns on me
I didn't just move into my forever home
But into my very own Whole Foods store

Finally Come Home

Ten hours

I was all alone

Ten hours

I was really bored

Ten hours

Until you finally came home

Only to walk right by me

And plop down on the couch

Only for me

To take a sharp swipe at your ankle

Now you're chasing me around the house

Now you're hobbling and cursing my name

Now I'm thinking these past ten minutes

Are the happiest I've been all day

Over Here!

Now I'm over here!

Now I'm on top of this!

Now I'm wedged between these!

Now I've torn through all of that!

Now my head is in this jar!

Now my butt is on this meal!

Now my body's in midair!

Now I'm flying through something dainty!

Now I'm hanging from your leg!

Now I'm hanging from the screen!

Now I'm hanging from a ceiling fan!

Now I'm in midair once again!

Now I'm outside!

Now I'm running back inside!

Now I'm hurtling back outside!

Now I'm on the roof!

Now it may not be your roof!

Now you're pleading with me to get off the roof!

Now I landed on your face!

Now I don't know

How I've been so many places

In the past minute and a half

But I do know that

Thanks to tracking litter

I can retrace my journey every single
  step of the way

Tell Them All

Tell my family

I love them

Tell my friends

I miss them

Tell the world

About the brave little kitten

Who tried to scale

The mighty stairs

Only to realize

That all of her mail

Will have to be forwarded

To the third step

For the rest of her life

Amuse Myself

Bat

Bat

Bat bat bat

Bat bat bat bat bat bat bat bat

Bat

Great

Now they're under the fridge

Well, time to see

If my person has a third set

For another round of house keys hockey

Ten

· · · · ·

One, two, three

Four, five, six,

Seven, eight, nine

And ten

Ten toes

All sticking out of your blanket

Ten toes

All quickly bitten

Ten toes

All clearly vanquished

Ten toes

Judging by their ungodly stench

All now very much dead

I Have a Collar

I have a little collar

With a little bell

That makes a little jingle

Jingle

Jingle

Jingle

Jingle

Jingle, jingle, jingle, JINGLE

I'm losing my mind

I can't hear myself think

When I run screaming mad

The jingles only get louder

I wish more than anything

I was covered in bugs

So I could just wear a flea collar

Like my lucky, filthy brother instead

Rainy Days

I love to gaze out the window

And see the clouds rally overhead

I love to press my nose against the glass

And smell the air before the storm

I love to tilt my head

And hear the tap tap tap

   of the drops on the ground

I love to gaze out the window

And know that at any moment

The dog will have to go out in that rain to pee

So Small

The sofa

The counter

The bookcase

You

Everything towers above me

Everything looms over me

Everything is so tall

And I feel so small

So wee

So less than a speck

That all I can do

Is take it out on the carpet

Right beneath my feet

HAHAHAHAHAHAHA!

Tiny, insignificant carpet fibers

That I soil daily

To you I must seem like a god!

Your Legs

. . . .

I weave and weave

Between your legs

I rub and rub

Against your legs

I roll and roll

Right by your legs

I hope and hope

It's just a phase

I beg and beg

It's just new urges

I pray and pray

It's not that I'm actually

Attracted to your legs

Because I've been here enough months to know

They're already in a committed relationship

   with the dog

Youth

The purpose of youth

The point of being young

Is to explore all that you can

Go as far as you can

Scale as high as you can

Reach what great levels you can

So long as you can

Always be in the vicinity

Of someone with a ladder or long arms

Adorable

. . . .

I curl my adorable fur body

Into an adorable fetal ball

As I tuck my adorable head

Into my adorable tail

And sigh my adorable sighs

As I rest adorably

Right on top of the one thing you need right now

Sleep, adorable me. Sleep.

I Pounce!

. . . .

I pounce on my brother!

He pounces on me!

Then I pounce on my brother!

Then he pounces on me!

Now I'm on top of him!

Now he's on top of me!

Aaaaaaaaaaaaand . . . time!

So with a score of 126-85

I win again!

Boy, how I do love to play

What I assume is Australian rules football

Dear Diary

Dear Diary

I ran, I ran

I ran, I ran

I ran, I ran

I caused something to shatter

I ran faster, I ran faster

I ran faster, I ran faster

I ran at blinding speed

I slept

I will always treasure this day

SAME OLD TROUBLE

It's a big, big world

And there are great people wherever you look

And if you play your cards just right

They will all leave you alone

OLDER CAT'S ADVICE

Gratitude

. . . .

Thank you

For everything

You do for me

Thank you

For everything

You have done for me

Thank you

For everything

You WILL do for me

Once I perfect hypnosis

Hero

· · · · · ·

Visionary

Revolutionary

Vanguard

Hero

These will be my names

These will be my legacy

These will be the chants

That will greet me

When I'm released from the bathroom

For my time out

As everyone agrees

Someone

Anyone

Had to end the tyranny

Of those hideous drapes in the den

Not Goodbye

. . . .

I still smell the older cat

On his favorite chair

On his favorite blanket

On his favorite toy

On me

I still smell the older cat

But I can't find him anywhere

And now his dish is gone

And now his bed is gone

And now you are crying

But I still smell the older cat

So tomorrow I will look again

Seen It All

. . . .

The couch

The bed

The chair

The sill

I thought I had sat

Everywhere this house had to offer

I thought I had seen

Everything this home had to give

I thought at my early age

I had lived my entire life

But then I saw the box

And now I sit inside the box

Staring off into the distance

Ignoring your pleas

To lift my ass so you can have

Just one of the chocolates inside

Even if it's one of the lemon-filled ones,
   you say
It's melting into your fur,
   you say
Please stop ruining Valentine's Day,
   you say
As I sit and lick my paw
Only to find the coconut one tastes
   kind of odd

You Did All This

. . . .

You did this
You did all this
When you left yesterday
When you came back today
When you left me alone all night
Sure, maybe those aren't your paw prints
Sure, maybe you didn't knock everything down
Sure, maybe you didn't put in the time and effort
To somehow unscrew a bookcase without thumbs
But I want you to look upon this wreckage
I want you to remember you abandoned me
And I want you to know that you did all this
And that I was but the forgotten innocent
Who just made damn sure it all got done

Give Him a Treat

. . . .

When the dog sits
You give him a treat
When the dog heels
You give him a treat
When the dog rolls over
You give him a treat
But when I run up the curtains so fast
That I slam my head against the ceiling
You just scream and scream and scream
Which leads me to conclude
That when the dog does something amazing
You think it's a trick
But when I do something amazing
You believe it's actually magic

Maybe I'm Confused

. . . .

Maybe I'm confused

Maybe I don't know any better

Maybe I was weaned too young

Maybe I bit down on your nipple too hard

But maybe you can calm down

And stop your constant screaming

Because, dude, I've only been sucking away

For maybe ten minutes tops

The Only Reason

. . . .

Listen to me

Believe me

Put your every confidence in me

When I say

That the only reason

I walked off

Right in the middle

Of you telling me your big news

Was so I could share it with
   the rest of the world

Stretch

. . . .

Stretch

Stretch

Streeeeeeeeeeeeetch

And still I'm too small

To take over the couch

So I knock down your lamp

To fill up its space

Wake me when it's time for bed

While You're Typing

I jump on your laptop while you're typing
And you just take me off
Then I jump on your laptop while you're typing
And you lift me off with a sigh
Then I jump on your laptop while you're typing
And you take me off with a grunt
Then I jump on your laptop while you're typing
And you yell, "Stop it!"
Then I jump on your laptop while you're typing
And you don't understand
That some writers just need editors
And others need to be told
"I'm sorry, but have you tried pottery instead?"

I Panicked

I panicked
I flinched
I lashed out
I drew blood
From the family dog's nose
I'm more monster than kitten
I'm more beast than pet
I'm being left alone
The dog is under the bed
I'm going to remember this trick

The Lap

. . . .

I want to be on your lap

I need to be on your lap

I have to be on your lap

I know you're currently standing

But my claws can only hold

On to your crotch for so long

So please take a seat

Because I want to be on your lap right now

Can't Stop

Ceiling

Wall

Floor

Wall

Ceiling

Wall

Floor

Wall

Ceiling

Wall

Floor

Wall

Please

Someone

Get me out

Of this rolling hamster ball

Sense of Wonder

Thanks to my sense of wonder

Thanks to my thirst for knowledge

Thank to my need to explore

To analyze

To learn

To find out all there is

About this new place I call home

Thanks to all that

And a poorly timed jump

I can confidently report

That everything you ever treasured

Should not have been placed

On a single shelf you installed yourself

A Mighty Roar

· · · · · · · · · · · · · · · · · · ·

I open my mouth

To release a mighty roar

But you just look at me

Smile and say, "Awwwww."

I open my mouth

To emit a resounding bellow

But then you just laugh

And say, "Who's my little fellow?"

I open my mouth

And to my horror hear my "Squeak!"

And now I realize why you don't know

I've been telling you off this entire week

We Both Know

Peace

Joy

Bliss

We both know in a moment

I'll be racing across the room

We both know in a moment

I'll be racing up the wall

We both know in a moment

I'll be causing your heart to pound

As I leave debris in my wake

But right now in this moment

In this second

In this space

Between my head and your chest

I want you to know

My heart is full

My world complete

My God, I'm happy

And now that we both know

Don't mind as I now dig

My claws into your torso

To help propel me to parts unknown

ACKNOWLEDGMENTS

....

This book—and almost everything I do—would not be possible without the tremendous love, support, and patience of my family, my friends, and all those cats who learned to share their innermost thoughts by learning how to type.

FRANCESCO MARCIULIANO is the author of the bestselling books *I Could Pee on This* and *I Could Chew on This*. He writes the internationally syndicated comic strip *Sally Forth* and the webcomic *Medium Large*. He was head writer for the Emmy award-winning children's series *SeeMore's Playhouse* and has written for Smosh and the Onion News Network. He is on Twitter at @fmarciuliano.